PIANO • VOCAL • GUITAR

JOURNEY

PIANO SHEET MUSIC ANTHOLOGY

Produced by
Alfred Music
P.O. Box 10003
Van Nuys, CA 91410-0003
alfred.com

ISBN-10: 0-7390-8621-9
ISBN-13: 978-0-7390-8621-6

CONTENTS

TITLE	ALBUM	PAGE
After All These Years	Revelation	30
Any Way You Want It	Departure	4
Anything Is Possible	Eclipse	10
Anytime	Infinity	20
Ask the Lonely	Frontiers	24
Be Good to Yourself	Raised on Radio	35
City of Hope	Eclipse	40
Don't Stop Believin'	Escape	54
Edge of the Moment	Eclipse	62
Faithfully	Frontiers	58
Girl Can't Help It	Raised on Radio	76
Good Morning Girl	Departure	73
Happy to Give	Raised on Radio	82
I'll Be Alright Without You	Raised on Radio	85
Just the Same Way	Evolution	92
Lights	Infinity	102
Lovin', Touchin', Squeezin'	Evolution	96
Only the Young	Frontiers	112
Open Arms	Escape	118
Patiently	Infinity	107
Send Her My Love	Frontiers	140
Separate Ways (Worlds Apart)	Frontiers	122
Stay Awhile	Departure	130
Still They Ride	Escape	134
Stone in Love	Escape	136
Wheel in the Sky	Infinity	150
When You Love a Woman	Trial by Fire	145
Who's Crying Now	Escape	156

ANY WAY YOU WANT IT

Words and Music by
NEAL SCHON and STEVE PERRY

Chorus:

Oh,__ she said, "An - y way you want it. That's the way you need it. An-

y way you want__ it." {She said, / I said,} "An - y way you want it. That's

the way you need it. An - y way you want__ it."

2. y way you want__ it."

8

ANYTHING IS POSSIBLE

Words and Music by
JONATHAN CAIN and NEAL SCHON

1. Up a - gainst the wall,

Chorus:

see how you i-mag-ine your life, you are what you dream, now, {then you / you} know that an-y-thing is pos-si-ble.

It's not who you are, it's where you wan-na go, you don't need a mir-a-cle. Be-lieve that

Bridge:

...end solo) It's not who you are,____ it's where you wan - na

go, you don't need a mir - a - cle.____ Be - lieve that

an - y - thing is pos - si - ble._____ It's time to

ANYTIME

Words and Music by
GREGG ROLIE, NEAL SCHON,
ROSS VALORY, ROBERT FLEISCHMAN
and ROGER SILVER

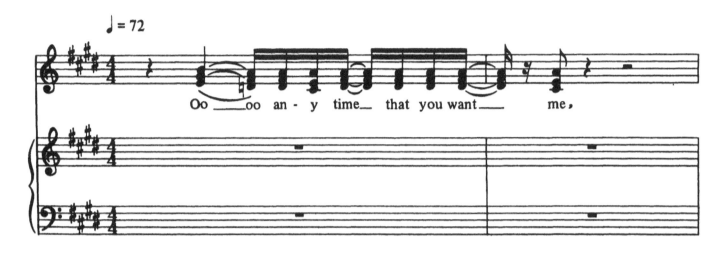

Anytime - 4 - 1

ASK THE LONELY

Moderately ♩ = 124

Words and Music by
JONATHAN CAIN and STEVE PERRY

Verse:

1. You've been picked and it's o - ver.___ What's___ that___
2. You've got some fas - ci - na - tion___ with___ your___

Ask the Lonely - 6 - 5

AFTER ALL THESE YEARS

Words and Music by
JONATHAN CAIN

*Original recording down 1/2 step in B.
**Vocals written at pitch.

After All These Years - 5 - 1

BE GOOD TO YOURSELF

Words and Music by
JONATHAN CAIN, NEAL SCHON
and STEVE PERRY

Verse:

1. Run-nin' out of self - con - trol,___ get-tin' close to an
2. When you can't___ give no more,___ they want it all, but you

Be Good to Yourself - 5 - 1

CITY OF HOPE

Words and Music by
JONATHAN CAIN and NEAL SCHON

Moderate rock ♩ = 104

City of Hope - 14 - 1

Verse 1:

1. Peo - ple wait - ing__ for some kind__ of sign from__ a-

bove.

44

Nev - er stop be - liev - ing, change will come.____

There's a

Chorus:

cit - y____ of hope be - yond_ all fears where

mir - a - cles hap-pen, where truth can be heard._ Don't you wan - na go

46

Verse 2:

2. On___ the edge of___ the world, a - cross o - ceans_ of___

___ blue,___

it's___ a place where_ a dream has a chance to___ come_

pain.

Nev - er stop be - liev - ing, change will come.

There's a

Chorus:

cit - y of hope be - yond all fears where

Nev - er stop be - liev - ing, change will come.___

There's a

Chorus:

DON'T STOP BELIEVIN'

Words and Music by
JONATHAN CAIN, NEAL SCHON
and STEVE PERRY

FAITHFULLY

Words and Music by
JONATHAN CAIN

Faithfully - 4 - 2

faith - ful - ly._____

2. Cir - cus

Oh,_____ oh,_____

oh._____

EDGE OF THE MOMENT

Gtr. tuned down 1/2 step:
⑥ = E♭ ③ = G♭
⑤ = A♭ ② = B♭
④ = D♭ ① = E♭

Words and Music by
JONATHAN CAIN and NEAL SCHON

Moderate rock ♩ = 116

Edge of the Moment - 11 - 1

Guitar solo ad lib.

Bridge:

C5   D5

Cb5   Db5

With your sweet love,   I   lose   all   track   of   time.___

C5   A5

Cb5   Ab5

I___   don't know   if   it's   day   or___   night.___

Guitar solo ad lib.

Repeat 3 times

GOOD MORNING GIRL

Words and Music by
MATTHEW SCHON and STEVE PERRY

Good Morning Girl - 3 - 1

GIRL CAN'T HELP IT

Words and Music by
JONATHAN CAIN, NEAL SCHON
and STEVE PERRY

Girl Can't Help It - 6 - 1

HAPPY TO GIVE

Words and Music by
JONATHAN CAIN
and STEVE PERRY

Happy to Give - 3 - 1

I'LL BE ALRIGHT WITHOUT YOU

Words and Music by
JONATHAN CAIN, NEAL SCHON
and STEVE PERRY

I'll Be Alright Without You - 7 - 1

Chorus:

(I'll be al - right___ with - out_____ you.___) Oo, there'll be

some - one else,_____ I keep tell-in' my - self._____ (I'll be al - right_ with - out_

Oh,___ love's an emp - ty place. I___ can still see your face.
___ you.___) (I'll be al -

right._____)

Guitar solo ad lib., repeat ad lib. and fade

JUST THE SAME WAY

Words and Music by
GREGG ROLIE, NEAL SCHON
and ROSS VALORY

Yes-ter-day___ was a good day,___ it's af-ter mid-night___ and I've got you on ___ my ___ mind.

Take a chance___ now the tim-ings' right.___ You're free to leave___ the key to ___ my ___ life.

me. ___ loves. ___
(Just the same way she loves. ___

loves. ___ Oh no, ___
loves. ___) Instrumental - - - - - -

___ you should be hold-in' on to him girl. ___ Oh, yeah ___ just like, just like you want to do. ___

___ Oh, no, ___ just love and squeeze him girl. ___ Oh, yeah, ___

LOVIN', TOUCHIN', SQUEEZIN'

Slow rock shuffle ♩. = 69

Words and Music by
NEAL SCHON and STEVE PERRY

1. You make me weep_____ and wan-na die,____ just when_ you said we'd try____ lov-in', touch-in', squeez-in'____ each

Chorus 1 (sing 1st time only):

Chorus 2 (sing 2nd time only):

Outro:

LIGHTS

Words and Music by
NEAL SCHON and STEVE PERRY

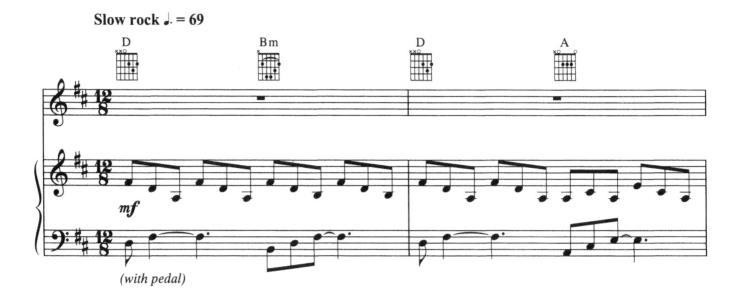

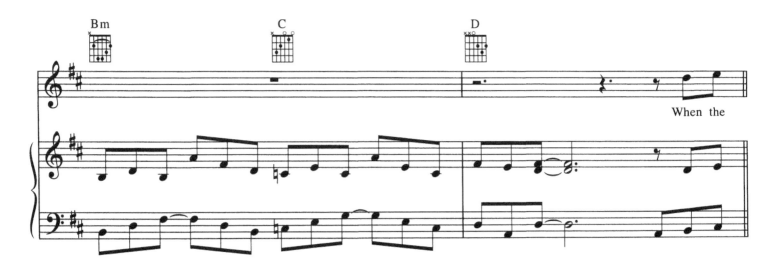

Chorus:

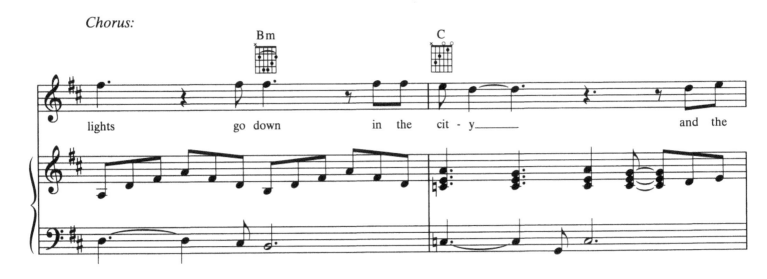

PATIENTLY

Words and Music by
NEAL SCHON and STEVE PERRY

ONLY THE YOUNG

Words and Music by
NEAL SCHON, JONATHAN CAIN
and STEVE PERRY

Moderately fast ♩ = 148

1. An-oth-er night in an-y town. You can hear the

Verses 2–4:

2. In the shad-ows of a gold-en age,___ a gen-er-
3. They're see-in' through the prom-is-es___ and all the
4. *Guitar solo ad lib.*

a-tion waits for dawn. Is it
lies they dare to tell.

Brave car-ry on; They
heav-en___ or hell?

bold and___ the strong.___ }
know ver-y well.___ }

young can say.

Only the young can say. Only the

young can say.

Repeat ad lib. and fade

OPEN ARMS

Words and Music by
JONATHAN CAIN and STEVE PERRY

Open Arms - 4 - 1

SEPARATE WAYS
(Worlds Apart)

Words and Music by
JONATHAN CAIN and STEVE PERRY

Moderate fast rock ♩ = 132

Verses 1 & 2:

1. Here we stand,___ world's a - part,___ hearts bro - ken in
2. Trou-bled times;___ caught be - tween___ con - fu - sion and

Separate Ways - 8 - 1

Bm7   G/C   D

If we can't go on_____ to sur-vive__
You'll nev-er walk a-lone._____ Take care,__

Am7   Bm7   G/C

____ the tide,   love____ di-vides._____
____ my love;   miss____ you, love._____ }

ff

Chorus:

Em   Em/D

Some-day love____ will find____ you. Break those chains____ that bind____ you.__

f

Em/C   Am7   D   D#dim

One night will____ re-mind____ you how we touched____ and went____ our sep - 'rate ways.

Lyrics:
If he ev - er hurts__ you, true love won't__ de - sert__ you.__

You know I_____ still love__ you though we touched__ and went__ our sep - 'rate ways.

our sep - 'rate ways.

STAY AWHILE

Words and Music by
NEAL SCHON and STEVE PERRY

Stay Awhile - 4 - 1

Fall in'. in'. Won't you just stay with me a-while?

2. (I'd sing,) any song your heart desires.
    I would sing out loud of love's sweet fires.
    Oo, I'd do all this and so much more
    If you'll just stay with me awhile.

STILL THEY RIDE

Words and Music by
JONATHAN CAIN, NEAL SCHON
and STEVE PERRY

Verse 3:
Traffic lights keepin' time;
Leading the wild and restless
Through the night.

Verse 4:
Spinning 'round, in a spell;
It's hard to leave this carousel.
'Round and 'round and 'round and 'round.

STONE IN LOVE

Words and Music by
JONATHAN CAIN, NEAL SCHON
and STEVE PERRY

Moderately

mp (2nd time guitar solo)

(end solo)

1. Those cra - zy nights, I do___ re - mem - ber___ in___ my
2. (see additional lyrics)

mf

youth.___   I do___ re - call, those were___ the

Stone in Love - 4 - 1

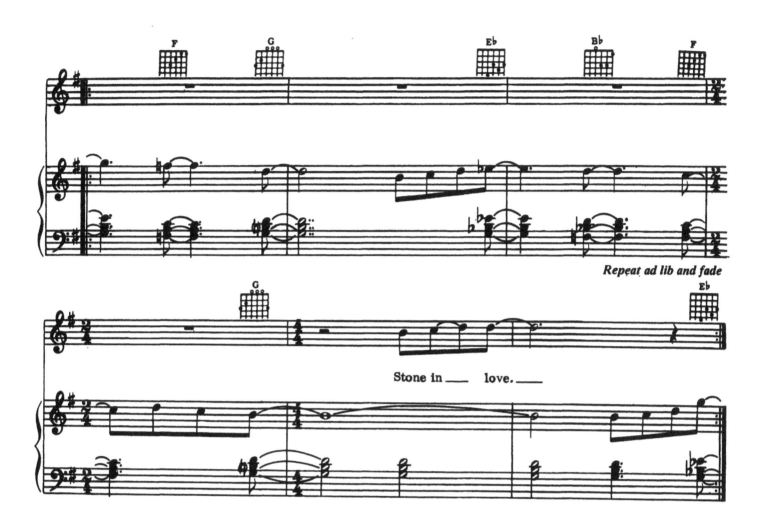

Repeat ad lib and fade

Stone in ___ love. ___

Verse 2:
Old dusty roads led to the river;
Runnin' slow.
She pulled me down, and in clover,
We'd go 'round.
In the heat with a blue jean girl;
Burnin' love comes once in a lifetime.
Oh, the memories never fade away;
Golden girl, I'll keep you forever.

SEND HER MY LOVE

Words and Music by
JONATHAN CAIN and STEVE PERRY

Moderately, expressively ♩ = 126

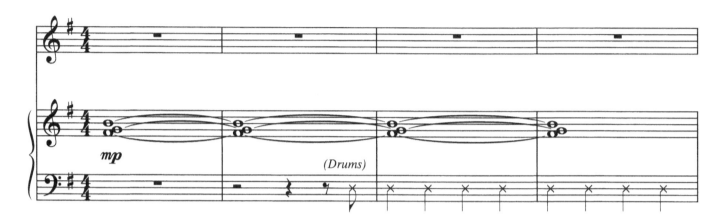

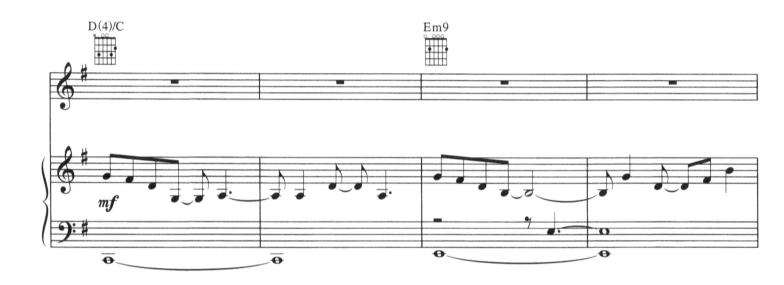

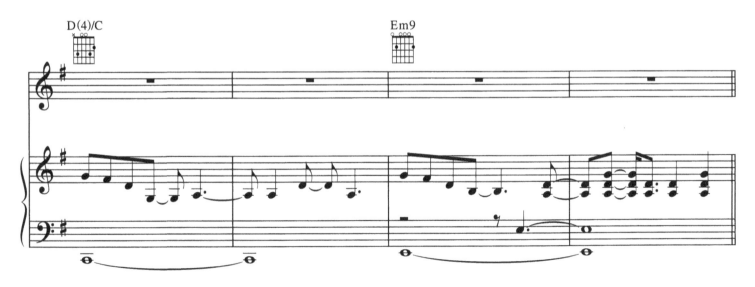

Send Her My Love - 5 - 1

I did-n't want to say___ good - bye.___
Bro - ken hearts can al - ways___ mend.___ }

Chorus:

Send her my love;___ mem - o - ries___ re - main.___ Send her my

love;___ ros - es nev - er___ fade.___

1.
Send___ her my love.___

2.
love.___

cresc.

f

cresc.

WHEN YOU LOVE A WOMAN

Words and Music by
NEAL SCHON, JONATHAN CAIN
and STEVE PERRY

*Original recording down 1/2 step in D♭.

When You Love a Woman - 5 - 1

146

WHEEL IN THE SKY

Words and Music by
NEAL SCHON, ROBERT FLEISCHMAN
and DIANE VALORY

1. Win-ter is here____ a - gain,____ oh Lord. Have-n't been home____ in a
2. I been try - in' to make it home.____ Got to make it be -

for to - mor-row.

Guitar solo ad lib.:

Ahh.

D.S. % al Coda

WHO'S CRYING NOW

Words and Music by
JONATHAN CAIN and STEVE PERRY

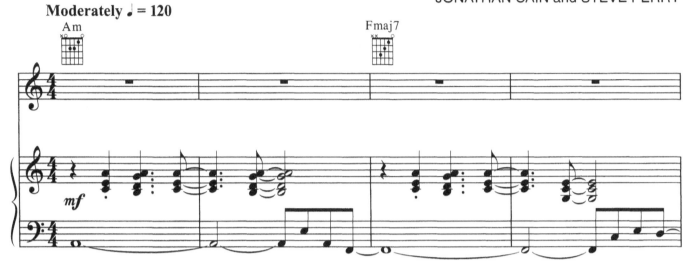

Verse:

1. It's been a mys - ter - y,_____ and still they
2. So man - y storm - y nights,_ so man - y

Who's Crying Now - 5 - 2

whoa.

D.S. ℅ al Coda

⊕ *Coda*

N.C.

Repeat *(Guitar solo ad lib.) and fade*